W9-APJ-340

TRIPP SCHOOL
850 HIGHLAND GROVE
BUFFALO GROVE, IL 60089

DISCARDED

DISCARDED

Peyton Manning

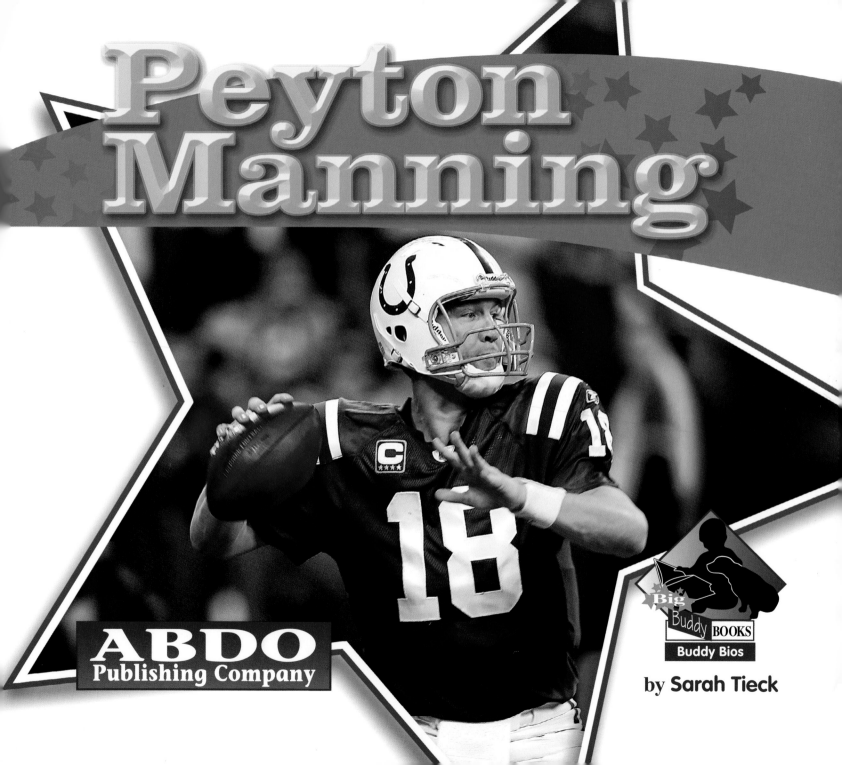

ABDO
Publishing Company

Big Buddy BOOKS
Buddy Bios

by Sarah Tieck

VISIT US AT
www.abdopublishing.com

Published by ABDO Publishing Company, 8000 West 78th Street, Edina, Minnesota 55439.

Copyright © 2011 by Abdo Consulting Group, Inc. International copyrights reserved in all countries. No part of this book may be reproduced in any form without written permission from the publisher. Big Buddy Books™ is a trademark and logo of ABDO Publishing Company.

Printed in the United States of America, North Mankato, Minnesota.
052010
092010
PRINTED ON RECYCLED PAPER

Coordinating Series Editor: Rochelle Baltzer
Contributing Editors: Heidi M.D. Elston, Megan M. Gunderson, BreAnn Rumsch, Marcia Zappa
Graphic Design: Maria Hosley
Cover Photograph: *AP Photo*: Kevin Terrell.
Interior Photographs/Illustrations: *AP Photo*: Chris Carlson (p. 23), Michael Conroy (p. 27), Darron Cummings (p. 23), Haraz N. Ghanbari (p. 27), Mark Humphrey (pp. 13, 15), Ben Liebenberg (p. 5), Erik Markov/Kokomo Tribune (p. 27), AJ Mast (p. 19), NFL Photo (p. 9), David J. Phillip (p. 29); *Getty Images*: Robert Caplin/Bloomberg via Getty Images (p. 21), Bill Frakes/Sports Illustrated (pp. 7, 11, 25), Patrick Murphy-Racey/Sports Illustrated (p. 13), Ezra O. Shaw/Allsport (p. 17).

Library of Congress Cataloging-in-Publication Data

Tieck, Sarah, 1976-
   Peyton Manning: famous quarterback / Sarah Tieck.
      p. cm. -- (Big buddy biographies)
   ISBN 978-1-61613-976-6
   1. Manning, Peyton--Juvenile literature. 2. Football players--United States--Biography--Juvenile literature. 3. Quarterbacks (Football)--Biography--Juvenile literature. I. Title.
   GV939.M289T54 2011
   796.332092--dc22
   [B]
                                2010013427

Contents

Peyton is considered one of the NFL's best quarterbacks. Quarterbacks are known for their passing skills. They often help their teams score.

Football Star

Peyton Manning is famous for his sports skills. He plays football in the National Football League (NFL). Peyton is a talented, popular quarterback for the Indianapolis Colts.

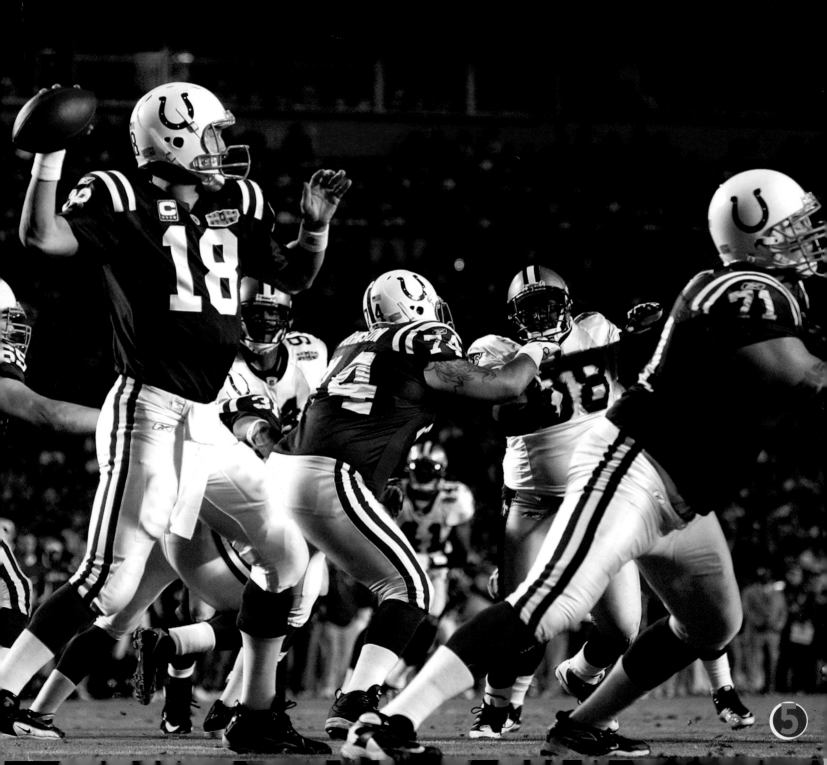

Family Ties

Peyton Williams Manning was born on March 24, 1976, in New Orleans, Louisiana. His parents are Archie and Olivia Manning. Peyton has two brothers. Cooper is older and Eli is younger.

Peyton (*bottom left*) is close with his family.

Arkansas

Mississippi

Texas Louisiana

New Orleans

GULF OF MEXICO

N
W E
S

Growing Up

Peyton spent his childhood in New Orleans. There, Archie played **professional** football with the New Orleans Saints.

Archie taught his sons how to play football. Peyton came to love the game while practicing with his father and Cooper. Together, they taught Eli to play.

Archie (*center*) was a professional quarterback from 1971 to 1984.

Did you know...

Football teams have several players for each position. The starters begin the game. Backups play if the starters are hurt or playing poorly.

School Years

Peyton attended Isidore Newman High School in New Orleans. He was a good student.

Peyton became starting quarterback of his high school's football team. He was soon the star player! During his last year in high school, Peyton received a national Player of the Year award.

Peyton (*above*) and Cooper played
football together at Isidore Newman.
Eli would later play on the team.

College Life

Many people wanted Peyton to attend the University of Mississippi after high school. His father had played football there. But, Peyton wanted to prove himself at another school. He chose the University of Tennessee. He began playing football there in 1994.

During college, Peyton studied speech communications and business.

Peyton did not play in many football games when he first started college. To prepare for when he would play, Peyton studied recordings of past games.

Did you know...

College football teams play bowl games after the regular season. The Gator Bowl is played each year in Jacksonville, Florida.

Partway through Peyton's first season, two University of Tennessee quarterbacks were injured. Peyton was asked to be the starting quarterback. He proved to be a strong player. Later that season, his team went to the Gator Bowl!

Peyton became known for having a strong throwing arm. For the next three years, he helped his team win many important games. He won awards for his talent on the field.

In 1997, Peyton received the Johnny Unitas Golden Arm Award. Outstanding college quarterbacks receive this award for having good character and leadership skills.

Did you know...

Peyton's brother Eli became a professional football player in 2004. He is the starting quarterback for the New York Giants.

Going Pro

After finishing college, Peyton decided to play **professional** football. So, he entered the 1998 NFL **draft**. The Indianapolis Colts got the first pick. They chose Peyton! This was a big honor.

Peyton's first season as an NFL player was 1998. Right away, he became the starting quarterback for the Colts.

Peyton has been a starting quarterback since he became an NFL player. This doesn't happen very often.

In the NFL, Peyton became known as a very hard worker. He helped his team succeed. The Colts made it to the **play-offs** in 1999, 2000, 2002, 2003, 2004, and 2005.

In 2004, Peyton broke records. He threw the most touchdown passes in one season. And, all the passes he threw that season added up to more than 4,000 yards. This was the sixth season in a row Peyton threw for that many yards!

Did you know...

A touchdown is a way to score points in football. It is worth six points.

In 2004, Peyton (*above*) threw 49 touchdown passes in one season. This broke a record held by Dan Marino. Dan was a famous Miami Dolphins football player.

Super Bowl Winner

The Colts had an exciting 2006 season. At the start, they played the New York Giants. This was the first time Peyton and his brother Eli played against each other. The Colts won!

Later that season, the Colts played in the Super Bowl. The Super Bowl is the championship game of the NFL. In a rainy game, the Colts beat the Chicago Bears 29–17! Peyton was named the Super Bowl's Most Valuable Player (MVP).

Did you know...

Peyton and Eli are friends off the field. They often talk about their work as quarterbacks.

At the Super Bowl, the winning team receives a Vince Lombardi Trophy. Vince was a well-known NFL coach. He coached the Green Bay Packers, who won the first two Super Bowls.

Did you know...

Many football players watch recordings of past games. This gives them ideas about how to beat other teams. It also helps them notice their strengths and learn from their mistakes.

In 2007, Peyton received an ESPY Award from ESPN. The award was for the best championship performance.

Peyton works hard to improve his skills. He practices with his teammates. And, he often watches recordings of past games.

People have noticed Peyton's talent. He was named the NFL's MVP in 2003, 2004, 2008, and 2009. He is the only NFL player to be named MVP four times!

MVPs receive a special trophy to honor their hard work.

Did you know...

In 2001, Peyton married Ashley Thompson. The couple lives in Indianapolis, Indiana.

Off the Field

   Family is important to Peyton. When he is not playing football, Peyton spends time with his wife, Ashley. He also golfs with his father and brothers.

Cooper, Archie, Eli, and Peyton (*left to right*) run the Manning Passing Academy. This four-day summer camp helps high school football players improve their skills.

Helping Hands

Peyton enjoys helping others. In 1999, he started the Peyback Foundation. This group helps children.

Peyton also works with his family to help others. In 2005, the Mannings helped Hurricane Katrina survivors in New Orleans. And, Peyton and Ashley have helped raise money to fight **cancer**.

Peyton Manning Children's Hospital

St. Vincent

Peyton helps St. Vincent Hospital in Indianapolis. In 2007, the children's hospital at St. Vincent was named for him.

Peyton spends time encouraging kids to be active.

Ashley and Peyton dress up and attend events together. Some of these events are to raise money for certain causes.

Buzz

Peyton has many fans.
People often take his picture.

The 2009 NFL season was one of Peyton's strongest. The Colts won their first 14 games. Peyton helped take his team to the Super Bowl in 2010. However, the New Orleans Saints won 31–17.

Peyton continues to work hard and succeed. Fans look forward to seeing what's next for Peyton Manning. They believe he has a bright **future**!

Did you know...

Peyton is known for his sense of humor. In 2007, he appeared on a comedy show called *Saturday Night Live*.

Snapshot

★ **Name**: Peyton Williams Manning

★ **Birthday**: March 24, 1976

★ **Birthplace**: New Orleans, Louisiana

★ **Turned professional**: 1998

★ **Plays with**: Indianapolis Colts

★ **Position**: Quarterback

★ **Number**: 18

Important Words

cancer any of a group of very harmful diseases that cause a body's cells to become unhealthy.

championship a game, a match, or a race held to find a first-place winner.

draft an event during which sports teams choose new players.

future (FYOO-chuhr) a time that has not yet occurred.

play-off a set of games leading to a final match to find a winner.

professional (pruh-FEHSH-nuhl) working for money rather than for pleasure.

valuable of great use or service.

Web Sites

To learn more about Peyton Manning, visit ABDO Publishing Company online. Web sites about Peyton Manning are featured on our Book Links page. These links are routinely monitored and updated to provide the most current information available.

www.abdopublishing.com

Index

TRIPP SCHOOL
850 HIGHLAND GROVE
BUFFALO GROVE, IL 60089